PUT ON YOUR
Dancin' Shoes

Written and compiled by

Liz Heaney

NEW LEAF PRESS
www.newleafpress.net

PUT ON YOUR

Dancin' Shoes

Published by
New Leaf Press/Master Books
Green Forest, Arkansas

Concept, production and design by
Left Coast Design
Portland, Oregon

Library of Congress Control
Number: 2002103018

All scriptures are taken from the King James
Version; the New American Standard Bible©,
the Lockman Foundation 1960, 1962, 1963, 1968,
1971, 1972, 1973, 1975, 1977; or are the author's paraphrase.

ISBN 0-89221-494-5

Contents

Acknowledgments

Many people helped to make this book a reality. I am grateful for their friendship, support, and expertise. My heart-felt thanks: to **Pat Edmonds** for the invitation to write this book; to **Jackie Edmonds**, **Heidi Ball**, **Shari MacDonald Strong**, **Traci Mullins** and my husband, **Casey Fast**, for reading and editing the manuscript and giving me valuable feedback; to **Kathy Vick** and **Bruce DeRoos** for finding just the right photos and for creating a design that helps my words dance; and to **Becky Griffo** and **Becky Morrell**, production assistants par excellence.

Chapter One

An Invitation

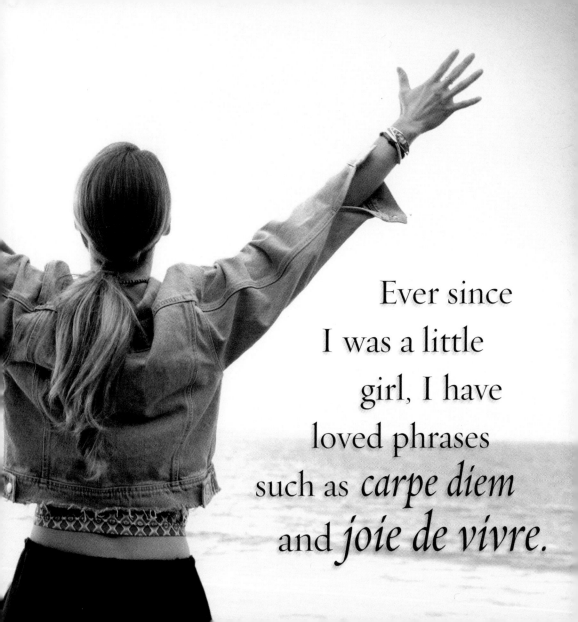

Ever since
I was a little
girl, I have
loved phrases
such as *carpe diem*
and *joie de vivre*.

Before I could pronounce the words, I understood the promise at their heart: life can be a dazzling, rich, and fulfilling dance.

Who wouldn't want a life like that? I know I do! I want to wake up each morning and put on my dancin' shoes. I want to live—really live. To be fully human and fully alive. I want to experience joy, to understand life's purpose, to engage in others' ups and downs, to live each moment in the awareness that God is good and takes delight in everybody, including me—and you.

Notice I said that's how I want to live; it's not how I actually live. At least, not most days. Far too often my life feels insignificant, a monotonous litany of tasks and responsibilities. Perhaps yours does too. That's why I decided to share with you the thoughts in this little book. Each one has helped me to remember that feelings and experiences are not to be feared or avoided; rather, they are what give my life richness. These thoughts remind me to listen to my heart, for that's how I can dance my way through the wonder of life.

Jesus said, "I am come that you might have life, and that you might have it more abundantly." Abundant life—that's what we can have, you and I. But it doesn't happen automatically. We have to choose it. So slip on your dancin' shoes and join me.

A friend loveth at all times.

THE BIBLE

Friendship A good friend is a connection to life—a tie to the past, a road to the future, the key to sanity in a totally insane world. LOIS WYSE

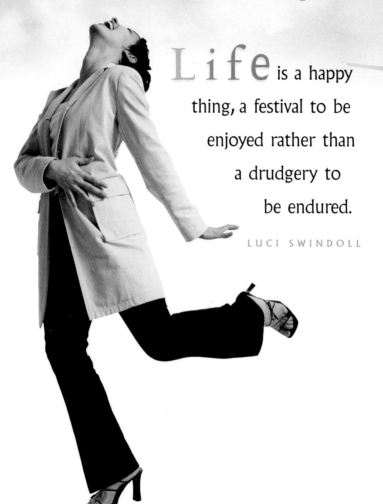

Life is a happy thing, a festival to be enjoyed rather than a drudgery to be endured.

LUCI SWINDOLL

Enjoying Life

Twenty years from now you will be more
disappointed by the things you didn't do than by
the ones you did do. So throw off the bowlines. Sail
away from the safe harbor. Catch the trade winds
in your sails. Explore. Dream. Discover.

MARK TWAIN

Good Health

I wish above all things that thou

mayest prosper and be in health.

THE BIBLE

Laughter

She who laughs, lasts.

MARY POOLE

If I'd known I was gonna $live$ this long,
I'd have taken better care of myself.

EUBIE BLAKE, AT AGE 100

Chapter Two

When we put
on our dancin' shoes,

Savor the Present Moment
we announce
our **willingness** to
embrace each
moment as a gift
from God,
bursting with
abundant potential.

When we make this choice we begin to recognize each moment as an opportunity to learn, to grow, to celebrate, to understand, or to rejuvenate.

We refuse to focus on regrets about the past or on worries about the future in order to be free to live in the moment, for this moment is all we have. We pay attention to what we are feeling and experiencing, whether pleasure or pain, and as a result we respond from our hearts in healthy and authentic ways.

When we live like this, we never get bored, because we are too engaged with life, too alive, to feel empty or restless. We have tuned our hearts to all that is rich and good in the world, which is so very, very much.

Begin savoring the present moment today by slowing down, literally. Make a decision not to pack your calendar so full. Take fifteen minutes to sit outside in the sun or near a warm fire and then think about all the people you love, and all those who love you. Open your heart to feel their love, and drink deeply from that well. Walk, don't drive, to the grocery store, cleaners, or coffee shop. Notice the colors of nature, breathe deeply and feel the sun or rain on your face. Enjoy simply being alive.

Joy

It isn't what you have, or who
you are, or where you are, or
what you are doing that makes
you happy or unhappy. It is what
you think about.

DALE CARNEGIE

Solitude

Only when one is connected to one's inner core is one connected to others. And, for me, the core, the inner spring, can best be re-found through solitude.

ANNE MORROW LINDBERGH

Love

There is only
one happiness
in life, to love
and be loved.

GEORGE SAND

When someone loves you, the way they say
your name is different. You know that your name
is safe in their mouth.   BILLY, AGE 4

Almost everything I know about *Be Positive* being **positive**, *I learned from my* husband, **Casey**.

He's one of the most up-beat people I know. He turns almost everything he does into a party—even conversations with phone solicitors. When they call, Casey doesn't hang up or bark at them; he cheerfully asks how they know him or me ("How else would you know our names?"). He asks diverting questions until the caller laughingly hangs up the phone. A good time is had by all.

Casey believes that if he loves someone, he should do his best to say yes when that person asks something of him. So when my mother calls and asks him to come over and help her with her computer, he doesn't hem and haw and make up excuses. He tells her he will, and he does. (No wonder she likes him so much.)

When I ask if he'll bring me coffee in bed, he says yes. And it doesn't matter that he doesn't drink coffee himself. He's this way, he tells me, because he'd rather enjoy than begrudge whatever it is that he's doing. It all comes down to choice, and he chooses to be positive.

In our quest to live well, to make life a dance to be enjoyed rather than a drudgery to be endured, you and I can do the same. When we do, we'll look on the bright side of inconveniences and annoyances. We'll think of all the reasons why we can do something instead of the reasons why we can't. We'll say yes to what brings joy to us and to those we love

Serenity

Don't get your knickers in a knot.

Nothing is solved and it just makes you walk funny.

KATHRYN CARPENTER

Without
enthusiasm
you are
doomed to
a life of mediocrity
but with
it you can
accomplish
miracles.

OG MANDINO

Optimism If you think you can, you can.
And if you think you can't, you're right.

MARY KAY ASH

Chapter Four

My friend
Shari wears
dancin' shoes.
A woman of
passion and
exuberance,
S-t-r-e-t-c-h *Yourself*
she often
*"grabs life by
the throat."*

She has a genetic heart condition, but she rarely stops at challenges

that are threatening, even something as heart-stoppingly frightening as bungee jumping. For her, jumping begged doing, simply because she had never done it before. It was a sample of the exciting things in life that might be missed without a s-t-r-e-t-c-h.

When Shari wasn't able to get pregnant, she pursued every route possible for having a child with her husband, including surrogacy. Despite the skepticism of some, she followed her heart. Her tenacity paid off when a childhood friend volunteered (yes, I said, *volunteered*) to carry a child for them.

You and I, if we want to live fully, must be willing to stretch ourselves beyond our comfort zones. What dreams have you felt unworthy to pursue? What have you been afraid to try? For me, the answer has been writing a book. For years I've been unwilling to try because of what people might think about my writing. I'm a successful editor, but writing is an entirely different game. Having my name on a book is a public display I have feared. But I can't tell you how good it feels to face my fear and write anyway. I may never win a Pulitzer, but I'm growing and learning. Come, join me and Shari in stretching ourselves.

Begin somewhere.
You cannot build a
reputation on what
you intend to do.

LIZ SMITH

dreams

Where there is no vision, the people perish. THE BIBLE

All of our d r e a m s can come true—

if we have the courage to pursue them.   WALT DISNEY

Intuition

We arrive at truth, not by reason only,

but also by the heart.

BLAISE PASCAL

Chapter Five

Move with the Rhythm

Do you want
to know a
secret for
living well?

It's understanding that life has a rhythm, and accepting that, as King Solomon put it, "To everything there is a season."

My friend Jackie knows all about life's rhythms. She has always loved dancing. When she married and had kids, the changes in her life meant that she could no longer continue her dance lessons—for the time being. But during the years of nightly feedings, potty training, and carpooling, Jackie never lost sight of her hope to study dance again. Then, the day finally came when her sons matured and she had more time for herself again. At age thirty-seven Jackie signed up to take ballet lessons.

After Jackie's first recital, her dance instructor gave each student a silk butterfly, describing how dancing is like taking flight. Jackie says, "I stood on the

stage, the only adult student, and realized that I've been like a butterfly in a cocoon, waiting many years to open my wings and take flight."

Throughout her life Jackie has dreamed of dancing in *The Nutcracker*. Last December she did. "My season to really dance is now," she observes. "I have received much joy in being a mom of three boys. Now I have that plus the joy of being a mom who dances!"

Once we accept our limits, we go beyond them.

BRENDAN FRANCIS

For each of us, life has a rhythm of its own. Some of us can do what we love throughout our entire lives, but others of us have to wait for another season. If we move with the rhythm and listen to the melody in our hearts, we'll find true freedom and a sense of purpose. Our spirits will soar. We'll stand confident, heads held high. The change we feel inside will be noticeable outside, as Jackie has discovered. She reports, "Since I've started dancing again, people have been asking, 'Have you grown taller?'"

So live that you
wouldn't be ashamed
to sell the family
parrot to the town gossip

WILL ROGERS

Other things may change us,
but we start and end with family.

ANTHONY BRANDT

Time

Time is the coin of your life. It is the
only coin you have, and only you can
determine how it will be spent. Be careful
lest you let other people spend it for you.

CARL SANDBURG

Chapter Six

While it's
possible to
dance alone,

Help Others Dance

most of us
would
prefer
having a
partner.

For one thing, partners allow us far greater variety in our dance steps. For example, one person can't do the Tango, but two can. And it takes a whole line of people to do the Tulsa Shuffle. Besides, dancing is simply more enjoyable with another.

So it goes with life: True joy comes from sharing with others.

Putting on our dancin' shoes means thinking about others: how we can help them or make their lives more enjoyable so that they too can join in the dance.

What might this look like?

My friend Traci intentionally likes to help others dance. That's why several years ago she volunteered to be a court advocate for neglected and abused children. Despite her full-time job and other commitments, Traci carved out several hours each month to be a voice for children who were unable to speak for themselves.

Judy, Traci's dearest friend, became temporarily incapacitated after falling on ice and breaking six ribs and damaging a lung. She was unable to work for five weeks and had to be on oxygen twenty-four hours a day. Traci gladly set aside her own needs to care for her friend. Judy's intense pain kept her from being able to move without help, but whether Judy needed assistance in getting dressed or going to the doctor, Traci stepped in to do what needed to be done, including helping her friend keep her sense of humor.

It never occurred to Traci to do anything else. Why? Because she wants her friend to dance again.

Giving Back

How lovely to think
that no one need wait a
moment, we can start now,
start slowly changing the world!

ANNE FRANK, AGE 14

The t r u e measure of a woman is h o w she treats someone who can do her absolutely no good. ANN LANDERS

Silent gratitude isn't much use to anyone.

GLADYS BROWYN STERN

A kindhearted woman gains respect.

THE BIBLE

Chapter Seven

It has been said, "Clothes don't make the man."

Be Disciplined

It can also be said that shoes don't make the woman—

even dancin' shoes! Dancin' shoes alone won't empower us to dance well... only discipline

and persistence lead to excellence. If we want to dance, we need focus and concentration. We must keep in shape and practice consistently.

The same is true for those of us who want to live well—to achieve our dreams, to have deeply satisfying relationships, to perform tasks with excellence, to be involved with things that matter. Discipline leads us to sit down and form a vision of how we want our lives to look. Discipline enables us to articulate the steps we need to take to move toward our goals, and then to take the steps, one by one. Discipline keeps us from giving up when we don't get what we want immediately or when others fail to believe in us. Discipline keeps our eyes on the goal and helps us to align our choices so that our vision becomes a reality. Discipline encourages us to say no to the things that will keep us from fulfilling our dreams.

Let's learn to love discipline, for it forms the foundation of the dance, and from it flows passion.

Perseverance It's how you deal with failure, not how you deal with success that determines who, in the end, really makes it. JANE PRATT

excel

Whatsoever thy hand
findeth to do, do it
with all thy might

THE BIBLE

1

When we do the best that we can, we never know what miracle is wrought in our life, or in the life of another. HELEN KELLER

Self-Discipline

All my life I've wanted to be somebody. But I see now I should have been more specific. JANE WAGNER

Chapter Eight

We *live* across the street from **Griffin** and **Mason**, two young boys.

Delight in Little Things

Little things delight them both.

When I walk into their house, Griffie who's two, toddles toward me, his face alight with

a big smile as he reaches up to me, calling, "Iz, Iz!" My husband and I often eat dinner in our kitchen nook that faces their house. When five-year-old Mason sees us there, he races out to their curb and totters on the edge yelling, "Casey! Liz! Can I come over?" Sometimes I invite him over to help me bake cookies, and it's as if I were offering him a trip to Disneyland. How happy it makes him!

Griffie and Mason understand what really matters in life. Little things like love and friendship fill them with joy.

Oh, to be so easily delighted! Things that can deeply satisfy and enchant the heart surround each of us, but we have to pay attention or they'll go unnoticed: the silky smoothness of a baby's skin, the sound of children laughing, the tender look of love in the eyes of our beloved, the taste of a fresh warm chocolate chip cookie. My friend Traci purchased some wind chimes because the sound makes her happy. I love to surround myself with lighted candles because of their cozy ambiance. They warm my heart on a dark, rainy day.

What little things delight you? Make a list to remind you to savor those things when they come across your path. Before you know it, you won't need a list. That's how this works, you see. When we put on our dancin' shoes, we grow in our awareness of simple wonders.

Success

When asked to name his greatest accomplishment in life,
he replied:"My children still come home to see me."

FORMER PRESIDENT
GEORGE H. W. BUSH

Life is what we make it.
Always has been, always will be.

GRANDMA MOSES

People are just about as happy

as they make up their mind to be.

ABRAHAM LINCOLN

Chapter Nine

Let Go of the Bad

Nothing
cripples our
ability to dance
more than an inability
or **refusal to let**
go of negative
feelings and
experiences.

Hold on to the Good

When we hang on to our hurt, refusing to forgive, or when we fail to challenge the lies we've been told ("You can't do that! You're not smart enough ...talented enough...disciplined enough..."), anger and bitterness will destroy our souls and kill our joy. If we want to experience the fullness life has to offer, we must let go of the bad, choosing instead to hang on to the good.

This past year I've watched Skye do just that. One by one, she has purposefully and painstakingly forgiven the people in her life who have caused her deep pain: a leader who had betrayed her by ostracizing her from a church she loved; an abusive ex-husband; an aunt who has made demeaning comments to her for years. When Skye let go of her pain and looked to God for help, she discovered an inner strength she didn't know she had.

But Skye didn't just wake up one morning and decide to forgive these people. Forgiveness was a process that took conscious work. It wasn't easy, but she did it. Skye's face is radiant as she talks about how good she feels. She laughs more. She talks about the joy she receives from holding her new grandson in her arms or from hanging out with her college-age daughter and her boyfriend. When I first met Skye, despair haunted her; but now hope often laces her words.

Skye dances a lot these days—and so will we if, like her, we let go of the bad and then focus on all that is good in our lives.

Hope I believe in the sun even when it's not shining.

I believe in love even when not feeling it.

I believe in God even when He is silent. UNKNOWN

Some people grow old before their time trying to look young after their time. UNKNOWN

Charm is deceptive
and beauty does
not last; but a woman
who fears the LORD,
she shall be praised.

THE BIBLE

Forgiveness Forgiveness is not saying that

the one who hurt you was right. Forgiveness is stating

that God is faithful and He will do what is right.

MAX LUCADO

Chapter Ten

Several years ago while trying to

Take Care of Yourself

mimic the moves of my friend from an avant-garde dance troupe, I ruptured my *Achilles tendon*.

In my exuberance I had taken a leap
and snapped the tendon. Upon landing, my

right foot could no longer support the weight of my body and I fell to the floor.

Suprisingly, I didn't have much pain, but I couldn't walk. I hopped to my car to drive home. Later a friend had to take me to the hospital where I had surgery the next day to reattach the tendon.

My doctor told me that my other tendon might rupture if I continued to engage in strenuous activity because my tendons are shorter than normal. This meant I could play it safe and refuse to run, ski or leap again, or I could begin to stretch those tendons every day and slowly build up my level of physical activity. I chose to stretch, and to keep on dancin'.

If we want to dance, we will take care of ourselves—physically, emotionally, intellectually, and spiritually—in order to prevent injuries and ward off self-doubt and exhaustion. We'll do what the doctors tell us: eat well, exercise regularly, and get plenty of rest. We'll balance the things we do for others with things we do just for ourselves; we'll sleep in, read a book, get a massage, or drink a cup of hot chai tea and honey. And we won't forget to stretch.

When we treat ourselves well, not only will we have fewer aches and pains, but we'll also feel better about who we are and what we have to contribute to the world. Our joy will bubble over into other areas. We'll walk with a dancer's stance: standing straight, chin up, chest open, shoulders back and down.

Confident. Full of hope. Ready to dance!

Purpose

The chief end of man

is to love God

and enjoy him forever.

WESTMINISTER CATECHISM

Chapter Eleven

The Perfect

A couple of years ago
Martha Williamson,
the *executive producer*
of the
Dance Partner hit
television show
Touched by an Angel,
co-wrote a book
called *Inviting God*
to Your Wedding.

She was getting married and wanted to create a wedding that involved God in a tangible, personal way.

"When God is there suddenly all your priorities are in order," she wrote. I agree.

When we make space for God—at our wedding or in our life—we acknowledge that someone greater than ourselves is in control of the universe and has our best interests at heart. We live in the awareness that God loves us and wants our partnership in making this world a better place. Such awareness opens our hearts and minds to see grace and wonder in everything good.

God, like a drummer, carries the beat for your dance and for mine. The rhythm is our unique expression—the unique talents and gifts and abilities given to us by the one who holds the beat. When we are in tune with that beat, when we listen to that "still small voice," we have the power to change, to become women of courage, grace, wisdom, passion and joy.

When we invite God to dance with us, we maximize our potential to be fully human, fully alive, fully awake ... to dance with all our hearts. After all, God is the Lord of the Dance.

What little things delight you? What makes you happy? Make a list, review it often and surround yourself with these things.

_____

_____

_____

_____

What are your dreams? What do you hope to do or accomplish in life? Start by identifying the steps that are necessary for you to reach your dreams—and pray for the courage to pursue them!

_____

_____

_____

_____

_____

What things might you need to let go of in order to participate fully in the dance of life? Ask God for the courage and grace to let go and to move on.

_____

_____

_____

How well do you take care of yourself? Do you get enough rest and exercise? Do you spend time regularly with people who inspire and strengthen you? Take stock of how you spend your time and identify what kinds of things are essential for your self-care.

_____

_____

_____

Who in your life encourages you to

put on your dancin' shoes? Make a lunch or coffee

date with that person and share what you've written on these pages.
Encourage them to join in the dance with you, and commit to supporting
each other.

_____

_____

_____

_____

_____

_____

_____

_____

_____

_____

_____

_____

Photo Credits